Teacher's Notes

Mozart's Magnificent Voyage

Based on the original work
by Douglas Cowling

Teacher's Notes written
by Susan Hammond

To Sarah and Katie,
who inspired this series

Published by The Children's Group Inc.
1400 Bayly Street, Suite 7
Pickering, Ontario, Canada L1W 3R2
For a complete catalogue, please call 1-800-757-8372
or e-mail moreinfo@childrensgroup.com
Visit us online at http://www.childrensgroup.com
© Classical Kids 1998 Mozart's Magnificent Voyage

Printed in Canada

CONTENTS

Letter to Teachers 3

How This Book Is Organized 4

Scene 1: Introducing the Cast 7

Horn Concerto, K. 495, Mvt 3 • Clarinet Concerto, K. 581, Mvt 2 • "Oragnia
Fitafagnia Fa" • Symphony No. 1, K. 16, Mvt 2 • Piano Sonata in F, K. 332, Mvt 3
• "We Are Three Spirits" ("Drei Knäbchen"), *The Magic Flute*, K. 620

Scene 2: Mozart's Young Life 14

Overture, *The Marriage of Figaro*, K. 492 • Child's Minuet in C • Symphony No. 1,
K. 16, Mvt 1 • Variations on "Là ci Darem" by Beethoven • "Evening Falls"
("Abendempfindung"), K. 523 • Flute Quartet, K. 285, Mvt 2

Scene 3: Italy and A Wedding 22

Symphony No. 40, K. 550, Mvt 1 • *Miserere Mei*, by Allegri • Cassation in C, K. 63
• Minuet, *Don Giovanni*, K. 527 • Barrel-Organ Variation on "Deh vieni," *Don
Giovanni*, K. 527 • Variations on "Ah, vous dirai-je, madame," K. 265 • Letter Duet
("Canzonetta sull' aria"), *The Marriage of Figaro*, K. 265

Scene 4: Conclusion 31

Eine kleine Nachtmusik, K. 525, Mvt 4 • Ave Verum Corpus, K. 618 • Waldstein
Sonata, Op. 53, by Beethoven • Piano Concerto in C, K. 459, Mvt 1 • Piano Sonata
in A, K. 331, Mvt 1 • Gran Partita, K. 361, Mvt 7 • "Blow Softly, You Breezes"
("Soave sia il vento"), *Così fan tutte*, K. 588 • Piano Sonata in A, K. 331, Mvt 1

Classical Kids and the Integrated Curriculum 37

Themes • Suggested Lesson Plan • Worksheet

Classical Kids Awards and Honors 40

LETTER TO TEACHERS

Mozart's life is a tale of childhood genius, musical triumph and personal tragedy. This recording tells the story through eyes of his seven-year-old son Karl. You will find here a double adventure — Mozart's short but magnificent life, and Karl's journey of understanding of himself, his father and the music that remains.

Recently, there has been an enormous upsurge of interest in this composer. First came the hugely successful play and movie *Amadeus*. Then came a veritable outpouring of scientific research into the beneficial effects of his music. Mozart makes you smarter. Mozart cures your body. Mozart soothes your soul.

Perhaps all these claims are true. But for young listeners, it is simply the story of a child traveling around the courts of Europe, dazzling adults with his incredible talents, that draws them. They marvel at a five-year-old who wrote minuets, an eight-year-old who composed symphonies, a twelve-year-old who conducted his own operas. Even for adults, these stories empower us, reminding us of the talents that live in all children, maybe not on Mozart's scale, but to be nurtured just the same.

Those who enjoyed *Beethoven Lives Upstairs* can meet here the man Beethoven admired above all others. Mozart was only 14 years older than Beethoven, but the two musicians were far apart in temperament. What took Beethoven many tortured sketches seemed to spill effortlessly from Mozart's pen. Beethoven was moody and isolated; Mozart was a social creature, a party goer, a jokester. Beethoven struggled with sums, Mozart delighted in mathematics. Beethoven spoke rough German, Mozart was fluent in four languages. Beethoven's childhood was truly terrible, Mozart's an unending adventure. Yet, for all that, the quality of their music, that which endures, is peerless in classical music.

Mozart just "works" for children and, not surprisingly, *Mozart's Magic Fantasy* remains one of Classical Kids' most popular recordings. His music is full of simple melodies, transparent orchestrations, infectious rhythms and heart-felt adagios. In *Mozart's Magnificent Voyage*, children learn of Mozart's adventuresome life story and his early death.

These Teacher's Notes are full of anecdotes that make Mozart leap off the pages of history books. Learn about Paris fashions in the late 1700s. Talk about pets, games and inventions. Sing or play Mozart's music. Compose a minuet. Open your ears and hearts and delight in one of humanity's greatest treasures.

A final note: Many teachers have concerns about using audio productions in the classroom, where the "fidget factor" cannot be tamed by "things to look at." Yet listening to recordings in class, like reading aloud, can encourage children to create whole worlds in their imaginations. This creative listening is one of childhood's greatests gifts, and is an essential skill for later life.

Let us give our children a window on earlier times, accompanied by glorious music, enticing drama and some profound themes.

Susan Hammond

HOW THIS BOOK IS ORGANIZED

Classical Kids recordings have been used in K–9 classes, but are most suitable for Grades K to 6. We have ranked the activities according to grade level with the symbols below. The icon applies to all the activities in the section, unless otherwise indicated. In the Exploring the Music sections, the icon also includes a number indicating the appropriate National Standard for Arts Education (see page 5).

 K–2   3–4   5–6   3–6   All

Presenting the Recording

This recording can be presented in its entirety (approximately 45 minutes), in two halves or in the six scenes outlined here. Each scene is identified in terms of tape time elapsed, CD track numbers and beginning and ending dialogue. You will find in these Teacher's Notes:

Getting ready: Questions and activities for use before the recording

Scene-by-scene suggestions: For use during the recording
- The story
- Music used in the scene
- Interesting background facts
- Discussion and activity suggestions
- Suggestions for exploring the music

Follow-up: Questions and activities for use after the recording
- Charts: Themes and skills, and a 10-day lesson plan
- Student's worksheet

Music in the Integrated Curriculum

Although Classical Kids recordings can be enjoyed as musical stories, our aim is to move children from being passive listeners to active participants: to engage their imaginations, to offer new skills and knowledge, to stimulate higher-order thinking skills and, finally, to give every teacher the tools to build a rich learning environment. These Teacher's Notes present more than 70 facts and thought-provoking questions to move beyond music into an integrated curriculum of social studies, creative writing, math, sciences and the other arts.

Our intent is to provide both specialists and general classroom teachers with engaging materials that expand their students' knowledge of music and times past. Instead of presenting a basal text of sequential musical skills, Classical Kids urges teachers and their students to "play with" musical concepts, to develop an interpretive vocabulary, to sing or play classical melodies on simple classroom instruments, to write lyrics, even to venture into composition. Children find it difficult to work in a vacuum, so let these recordings serve as a model, captivating young listeners with a moving story and then motivating them to acquire new facts and skills. Put these recordings in your classroom library for repeated listening.

Classical Kids and Children with Special Needs

Classical Kids recordings do not talk down to children. Our challenge here has been to design concrete activities that are sufficiently broadly based to inspire and involve children with special needs.

Teachers of children with learning disabilities often use the activities designed for younger classes, or allow more time for tasks: retell the story, dance, draw, sing or clap. Those teaching children with physical disabilities concentrate on singing, storyboarding, drawing or discussing events from the past. Teachers of children who are deaf or hard of hearing can tell the compelling story of Beethoven's triumph over deafness in *Beethoven Lives Upstairs*.

ESL students benefit from recordings that use well-spoken English to promote oral comprehension. Singing and writing lyrics are also wonderful ways to learn a second language. Classical Kids materials are available in other languages. Illustrated books of *Beethoven Lives Upstairs* and *Tchaikovsky Discovers America* are available in Spanish, and recordings of *Beethoven Lives Upstairs* and *Vivaldi's Ring of Mystery* are available in French.

The Teacher's Notes in this series encourage gifted students to write variations, study rondo structure, venture into European history and write time-travel stories with shifting points of view.

To all students, we encourage you to ask: "Who would want to do the possible all your life? The *impossible* — that's exciting!"

Assessment

Assessment in the arts is always difficult, often subjective, yet ultimately essential to spur excellence. Depending on what you hope to achieve with your arts program, you can test students individually or in groups, orally or on paper, for skills or understandings. These Notes encourage children to form their own questions, define tasks, discover research strategies, justify interpretations and then create a final product. Each of these stages can be assessed by the teacher. A sample student worksheet is included at the end of this book.

Observe and assess your students not only on final results but also on the care taken with the process. We encourage specialists to move beyond traditional music skills into cultural history, creative writing, research projects, time lines, story boards, set designs, murals or dance. Conversely, general classroom teachers are urged to try musical activities not necessarily based on playing proficiency. These listening and interpretive skills are important for music and for life in general.

Exploring the Music with Classical Kids

The suggested activities in the Exploring the Music sections are coded by number to reflect how they fulfill the U.S. National Standards for Arts Education.

1. *Singing, alone and with others, a varied repertoire of music.* Classical Kids believes that singing is primary for all music-making. The series offers more than 40 classical songs written out, and students are encouraged to write their own lyrics to well-known orchestral pieces and sing them.
2. *Performing on instruments, alone and with others, a varied repertoire.* These Teacher's Notes offer more than 50 pieces written out for recorders, glockenspiels, piano or guitar.

3. *Improvising melodies, variations and accompaniments.* The series encourages actively "playing with" musical elements, making answering phrases in ABA form, creating melodies based on chords and scales, and improvising variations or canons.

4. *Composing and arranging music within specified guidelines.* Be it creating "music from Neptune," writing ragtime, superimposing melodies, or composing music over which to read script, we seek to fire a child's musical imagination.

5. *Reading and notating music.* All the written-out pieces can be photocopied for classroom reading. Some titles include step-by-step descriptions for learning to read notation.

6. *Listening to, analyzing and describing music.* Musical terminology, instrumentation and form are explained. We encourage students to graph the "musical spine" of scenes in terms of tempo, instrumentation and mood. Classical Kids is particularly interested in helping students develop a descriptive vocabulary to interpret and listen to music imaginatively.

7. *Evaluating music and music performances.* All the music on the recordings has been expressly recorded to reflect images in the script. This provides an opportunity to talk about the performances and compare them to other recordings of the same piece.

8. *Understanding relationships between music and the other arts as well as disciplines outside the arts.* Classical Kids offers something unique for the last two criteria (8 and 9). The Discussion and Activities sections link music to other arts and subjects.

9. *Understanding music in relation to history and culture.* In the Background section of every scene, the music is set in its historical context. You will find a wealth of anecdotal facts and vivid descriptions of the times, without having to go to a library for outside sources.

(Adapted from National Standards for Arts Education *published by Music Educators National Conference. Copyright 1994. Reproduced with permission. The complete National Standards and additional materials related to the standards are available from Music Educators National Conference, 1806 Robert Fulton Drive, Reston, VA 22091.)*

Synopsis of the Story

The Dream Children are about to be written out of Mozart's most famous opera. In the hopes of changing their fate, they enlist the help of the composer's young son Karl. Together the children embark on an incredible journey that takes them back in time to Mozart's childhood as well as far into the future. Along the way, Karl learns much about his father and comes to understand his legacy of timeless music.

Things to Talk About Before the Recording

- Have you ever sat at the top of the stairs looking down on a grownup party? Imagine floating over Europe in a magic boat, invisibly spying on the scenes below. This is what Karl and the Dream Children do in this recording.
- Can you name a child prodigy in the arts or sports? Do most prodigies continue to shine into adulthood?
- Do you know that Mozart had two sons? Can you name children of famous people who have continued in their parents' profession?
- Looking at the cover, what do you think might happen in this recording?

SCENE 1: INTRODUCING THE CAST

LENGTH OF SCENE: 8:57   TAPE STARTING POINT: SIDE 1/0:00   CD TRACKS 1–5

BEGINS: *"Rehearsal's over, Fritz. Off the stage!"*
ENDS: *"All right, let's go!"*

The Story

After a rehearsal, the three Dream Children are playing in the flying boat from *The Magic Flute*. They decide to spy on Mozart in his summer hut. Mozart writes a letter to his wife, Constanze, about his decision to cut the Dream Children out of his opera. He talks about the problems he's having with their seven-year-old son, Karl, and his intention to visit the boy at school to straighten him out. As the stage boat becomes "real," it takes the Dream Children off to find Karl, who is furious at being sent to a boarding school far from his family. The Dream Children try to enlist Karl's help in saving their role in the opera. He decides to join them on their magic boat.

The Music

- Horn Concerto, K. 495, Mvt 1
- Clarinet Concerto, K. 581, Mvt 2
- "Oragnia Fitafagnia Fa"
- Symphony No. 1, K. 16, Mvt 2
- Piano Sonata in F, K. 332, Mvt 3
- "We Are Three Spirits" ("Drei Knäbchen"), *The Magic Flute*, K. 620

Background Information

Who Are the Dream Children?

Those of you familiar with the Classical Kids recording *Mozart's Magic Fantasy* will recognize the Dream Children as the Three Boys who led Prince Tamino to Sarastro's Castle (Track 9). Mozart specified three boy sopranos for his opera; today girls often sing one of the roles.

Who Was Karl?

Mozart's son Karl was born on September 21, 1784. At the tender age of three, he was sent away to boarding school, returning to Vienna only for school holidays. A visitor to their house described a charming picture of Mozart composing while his wife cut quill pens for the copyist and Karl wandered around the garden singing. Only seven years old when his father died, Karl grew up to be an accountant in northern Italy.

Karl's younger brother, Franz Xavier, was born in the summer of 1701 while Mozart was writing *The Magic Flute*. When his father died, he was only five months old, and grew up to become a minor composer, curiously using the pen name of Wolfgang Mozart.

Mozart's Family and Early Life in Salzburg

- **Life:** Mozart was born on January 27, 1756, at 8 p.m. in Salzburg, Austria. He died of liver failure in Vienna on December 5, 1791, just before 1 a.m., not quite 36 years old.
- **Name:** It was common for children to have many names. Mozart had five: Johannes (his grandfather), Crysostomus (his Saint's name day), Wolfgang (after Lake Wolfgang where his mother was born, and after his maternal grandfather), Theopholis (after his godfather; he later preferred the Italian form of this name, Amadeus), Mozart.
- **Father:** Leopold was a composer, musician and teacher who spent much of his life promoting his son's career. He also wrote many pieces for students, several symphonies and a book on how to play the violin that has been translated into many languages.
- **Mother:** Anna Maria was a kindly Salzburg matron with a keen sense of humor. She must have been an intrepid traveler, packing, cleaning and pressing court clothes for three years during the Grand Tour (see Scene 2).
- **Sister:** Like Felix Mendelssohn, Mozart had a sister five years older than he was. Anna Maria Mozart, affectionately known as Nannerl, was also a child prodigy. She played the harpsichord brilliantly and, according to her brother, composed quite well. Although these pieces have been lost, her travel diary (written in four languages) was not. At 15, she was taken off the concert circuit to stay at home, but she and her brother exchanged affectionate letters, usually ending with "I kiss you a thousand times." After Mozart's marriage to Constanze, the siblings drifted apart when Nannerl stayed home to teach and look after Leopold's household. Nannerl did not attend Mozart's funeral, and kept very closemouthed about her brother. She died on October 29, 1829, at the age of 78.
- **House:** The Mozart family lived on the second floor of a house in Salzburg. The main rooms overlooked a courtyard with a community well, from which the children drew water. The family was well known, and in fact no address was needed to send them a letter. The landlord, Lorenz Hagenauer, had a boy about Mozart's age. Lorenz received many letters from Leopold describing the Grand Tour.
- **Character:** Mozart was described as having a "lively disposition for every childish pastime and prank." Music filled his life, whether he was riding a hobby horse down the hall or insisting that toys be returned to their places, while loudly singing a march.

Discussion and Activities

Mozart's Pets

Mozart kept pets all his life. As a child, he even had a pet grasshopper, but he was primarily a dog person (he had three, named Bimperl, Goukerl and Katherl). Fond of birds, he once trained a pet starling to whistle the Rondo of the Piano Concerto No. 17. He was heartbroken when the bird died, and led a solemn funeral procession into the backyard to bury it.

Questions to ask:
- Do you have any pets?
- What special qualities do you like in them?
- Would you choose a dog over a cat? A fish over a rabbit? Why?

The Magic Boat and Time Travel

Two hundred years ago, "magic operas" thrilled Viennese audiences with their special effects like rivers of fire, trap doors and suspended stage "machines" (like the flying boat!).

Questions to ask:

- Have you ever been to a live musical? Describe some of the staging effects.
- Draw your impression of the boat arriving with "its sails sparkling in the moonlight."
- *Mozart's Magnificent Voyage* uses the flying stage boat from *The Magic Flute* to travel through space and time. Can you name a book or movie based on time travel?
- Can you think of some problems that time travel can pose for producers? [Answer: inventive transport devices, believability and clarity of plot.]
- What other devices for time travel have you found in books and movies? [Answer: a musical sound or lighting effect, an object to hold, a hidden door to walk through.]

Casting and Vocal Technique

The children on this recording were discovered through an advertisement in the newspaper saying, "Classical Kids needs kids." We wanted to find children with untrained, believable, non-commercial voices.

Questions to ask:

- Have you ever heard your voice on tape or video?
- As you listen to the children on this recording, pretend you are a casting director and analyze their diction and interpretation. Are the voices clear, lisping, raspy, high, excitable, calm? What peculiarities do you notice?
- Now tape and listen to yourself singing and talking — notice the rise and fall of your own voice, any good or bad habits, and favorite phrases. (Mozart's was "Superlatte!")

Sound Effects and Pictures in the Mind

Questions to ask:

- Sound effects are to recordings as what are to movies? [Answer: special effects. Both create a sense of space.]
- Sound effects are wonderful for creating pictures in the mind. Find the five examples in this first scene. [Answer: bell, crickets, owl, wind, slamming door.]

Life without School

It was not until the late 1800s that children were expected to go to school. Ask students:

- How would you spend your time if you did not have to go to school?
- What talent or interest would you develop?

Exploring the Music

The Horn Concerto

This opening Horn Concerto is an irrepressible romp in 6/8 time. It is like a patter song. Activities to suggest:

- Count aloud a quick six beats while stamping your feet on beats one and four (1–2–3–4–5–6).
- Make up your own lyrics to the Horn Concerto. Alternatively, sing it with these words:

> *Oh bring me a horn now, and then I shall play it,*
> *Please don't shut the window, I want you to stay.*
> *I know that my playing is driving you crazy,*
> *The dog and the cat, they are running away.*
>
> *I love my horn, though my lips they are burning, my cheeks so sore,*
> *Please bring my horn, I can't get it through the door.*

The Clarinet Quintet

Almost any recording of Mozart "hits" includes this slow movement from the Clarinet Quintet. It quickly settles a busy classroom, so keep a copy handy! Analyze this movement with your class by asking these questions:

- Does the melody sound major or minor? [Answer: it sounds minor because it is slow, but it is actually major.]
- The mood is often called sad. Do you agree? Suggest other adjectives. [Examples: haunting, lonely.] How is this mood achieved? [Answer: slow tempo, clarinet timbre, soft.]
- Describe the accompaniment. [Example: gently rocking strings.]
- Does the clarinet theme walk from one adjacent note to the next, or does it hop in expressive intervals? [Answer: intervals.]
- How does the violin come in? [Answer: in a contrary motion, drifting down as clarinet reaches up.]
- Select the musical term for tempo: allegro (lively) or adagio (slow) or moderato (medium)? [Answer: adagio.]

"Oragnia Fitafagnia Fa": A Bedtime Song

Mozart often said he would keep his father in a glass jar so that he would never die. When he was four, he wrote this little nonsense song for his father. Mozart would stand on a chair to sing it with his father, then kiss him on the nose and go to bed.

- Teach this song to children as young as four. Sing it first in unison and then as a round.
- Suggest that your students make up their own words and sing them.

Oragnia Fitafagnia Fa

O - rag - nia   Fi - ta - fag - nia   Fa, Ma - ri - na   fa,   Ga - mi   na - Fa

O - rag - nia   Fi - ta - fug - nia   Fa, Ma - ri - na   fa,   Ga - mi - na - Fa.

O - rag - nia   Fi - ta - fag - nia   Fa, Ma - ri - na   fa,   Ga - mi   na - Fa

"Oragnia Fitafagnia Fa" is similar to the opening bars of "A Girlfriend" from *The Magic Flute,* written in 1791. Apparently, Mozart started and ended his life with the same melody: a musical circle of life.

- Ask the class to sing the melodies and identify the similarities. [Answer: up a fourth, then adjacent notes in the same shape.]

A Girlfriend

Symphony No. 1, Second Movement

Questions to ask:

- How does this slow movement suggest the flying boat? [Answer: theme floats on triplets.]
- What instruments carry the melody? [Answer: French horns.] When he was eight in London, Mozart was particularly impressed with the English horn players.
- What are the violins playing? [Answer: repeated murmuring triplets.]

- Divide the class in two sections. Have one group clap the triplets while the other claps the eighth notes. Playing three against two beats is harder than you think!
- Mozart used this childhood theme in the closing of his last symphony (Symphony No. 41, "The Jupiter," K. 551). Another musical circle. Sing the first four notes of the horn theme.

Symphony No. 1

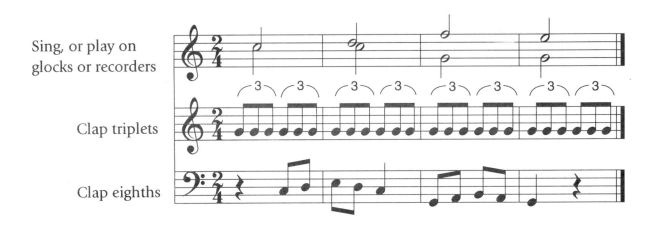

"Drei Knäbchen"

This transparent music is sung by the three sprites in *The Magic Flute* as they lead Tamino to Sarastro's castle.

- Ask the children to describe this piece. What is its mood? [Answer: floating, magical.]
- What is its instrumentation? [Answers: plucked strings, oboes in thirds.]
- Sing it as written here.

Drei Knäbchen

We are three spi-rits come to save you; The time is short, a
jour-ney a-waits you. Oh join our quest, we'll tra - vel on, Into a dream that's
past and gone. Come sail with us, come, sail with us.

SCENE 2: MOZART'S YOUNG LIFE

LENGTH OF SCENE: 9:52   TAPE STARTING POINT: SIDE 1/8:57   CD TRACKS 6–10

BEGINS: *"Let's go! Climb aboard, we're sailing!"*
ENDS: *"You're the little boy with the whole world of music in your head."*

The Story

The magic boat takes the children over 18th-century Europe towards England. It lands at the court of Queen Charlotte, where eight-year-old Mozart is conducting his first symphony. The Queen teases Mozart about proposing to the Queen of France. She also refers to King George III's problem with his colonies in America. In a tender bedtime scene, Mozart's mother sings a lullaby and Leopold tells his son a bedtime story.

The Music

- Overture, *The Marriage of Figaro*, K. 492
- Child's Minuet in C
- Symphony No. 1, K. 16, Mvt 1
- Variations on "Là ci Darem" by Beethoven
- "Evening Falls" ("Abendempfindung"), K. 523
- Flute Quartet, K. 285, Mvt 2

Background Information

The Early Tour (Mozart at Five)

Mozart and his sister were taken by Leopold to perform for the Empress Maria Theresa at her palace in Vienna. When the little boy slipped on the shiny marble floors, Princess Marie Antoinette, only a year older him, helped Mozart get up. He charmingly proposed marriage to her. The Empress rewarded Mozart and his sister with the exquisite lilac silk outfits you can see in many books on Mozart.

The Grand Tour (Mozart from Six to Nine)

Imagine being away from home for three and a half years! Leopold gallantly led his family through the courts of Europe, leaving on June 9, 1763, and returning in November 1766 — Mozart left Salzburg a six-year-old prodigy and returned a nine-year-old composer. This scene includes details of this extraordinary adventure:

- Nicknamed "the little magician," Mozart could perform and improvise any piece of music set before him. He could play the harpsichord with the keys covered and his hands crossed. He had perfect pitch and could name notes from several rooms away. So astonishing were his abilities that people pinched him to see if he was real!
- Traveling conditions were appalling. Leopold's letters describe "the pitching motion of heavy wheels, broken axles, the thumping of 16 large hooves" and filthy hotels with "bugs, fleas, rats, clouds of flies, traces of old food, dirty linen."
- The Mozart family were like a traveling band today. They had to transport a clavichord, two violins, cases of music, bulky boxes of clothes all strapped to the coach roof, and rugs or blankets to keep warm. Once, Mozart played a minuet to charm a customs officer at one of the innumerable border crossings.

- The first important stop was Versailles, *France*. In the enormous 200-room palace of Louis XV, blasts of frigid air blew along the mirrored marble passages, up the stately staircases and along stinking back passages. Wine froze on the tables. People kept themselves warm with furs and lap dogs, which befouled silk gowns and palace corners. In summer, ladies in tight corsets and heavy silk dresses swooned in the heat.

- At the New Year's Eve feast, young Mozart was honored to stand behind the Queen's chair and eat off her plate. The family was amazed at the rigid formality of the French court: the three-hour-long dinners and rules that everyone rise, pray, sleep and eat at the same time as Louis XV.

- The family loved being in *England* so much that they stayed for 15 months. They enjoyed the informal court of George III and Queen Charlotte, and the many performance opportunities offered by this great musical city (see Leopold's letters below).

- While in London, eight-year-old Mozart befriended Bach's youngest son, Johann Christian, then in his twenties. Mozart sat on Bach's lap and played the organ with him. They remained life-long friends.

- After leaving England, the family was eager to get back to Salzburg. The journey home was often delayed by illness. Leopold describes Nannerl almost dying of typhoid fever in *Holland* (see below). Then Mozart caught the disease and spent nine days barely conscious "without speaking a single word."

Little Wolfgang has contracted an illness which in four weeks has made him so wretched that he is not only absolutely unrecognizable, but has nothing left but his tender skin and his little bones. For the last five days, he has been carried daily from his bed to a chair. Yesterday and today, however, we led him a few times across the room so that gradually he may [once more] learn to use his feet and stand upright by himself... It began with a fever. Our night vigils were shared, as they were during my daughter's illness, so that it is owing to the great grace of God that we, especially my wife, have been able to stand all this... Expense must not be considered. The devil take the money, if one only gets off with one's skin!

Dear Lorenz,
I greatly fear for my daughter... Nannerl is [sick with typhoid and] delirious, talking in her sleep, now in English, now in French and now in German. And as our travels have given her plenty to chatter about, we often had to laugh in spite of all our distress. We divide the time at midday, each of us sleeping about five or six hours.

P.S. My wife and I, Nannerl and our all-powerful Wolfgang send greetings to you, to your whole household and to all of Salzburg.

Dear Lorenz,
Wolfgang is extraordinarily jolly, but a bit of a scamp as well. And Nannerl no longer suffers by comparison with the boy, for she plays so beautifully that everyone is talking about her and admiring her execution.
(Anderson, page 39)

To all Lovers of Sciences.

The greatest Prodigy that Europe,
or that even Human Nature
has to boast of, is,
without contradiction,
the little German Boy,
WOLFGANG MOZART;
a Boy, Eight Years Old,
who has and indeed very justly,
raised the Admiration
not only of the greatest Men,
but also of the greatest Musicians
in Europe.
It is hard to say, whether his
Execution upon the Harpsichord
and his playing and singing at sight,
or his own Caprice, Fancy, and
Compositions for all Instruments,
are most astonishing.
The Father of this Miracle,
being obliged by Desire of
several Ladies and Gentlemen
to postpone,
for a very short time,
his Departure from England,
will give an Opportunity
to hear this little Composer
and his Sister,
whose musical knowledge
wants not Apology.
Performs every Day in the Week,
from Twelve to Three o'clock
in the Great Room,
at the Swan and Hoop, Cornhill.
The two Children
will play also together
with four hands
upon the same Harpsichord,
and put upon it a Handkerchief,
without seeing the Keys.

Reassessing Leopold

Although Leopold has often been depicted as an unfeeling tyrant who exploited his son's talents, his letters tell a different story. It was Leopold's superlative teaching abilities that nurtured Mozart's incredible output of music. On tour, Leopold willingly shared parenting duties with his wife.

Discussion and Activities

Science: Disease in the 1700s

In the 1700s, breastmilk was considered unhealthy, so babies in Salzburg were fed water drawn from polluted wells, which was sweetened. Leopold and his wife lost five babies, leaving only Wolfgang and Nannerl. Wolfgang and Constanze in turn lost three babies, with only Karl and Franz Xavier surviving.

• Ask students what nutrients were missing from this infant diet.

While in London, Leopold caught "a kind of native complaint which they call a 'cold'." Before all of today's cough syrups and decongestants, bed rest was the only answer to this potential killer. Discuss these theories with your class:

• Feed a fever, starve a cold.
• You can catch a cold from breathing the night air.
• You can cure pneumonia by bloodletting with leeches on the skin.
• A cold is a viral infection.
• A cold is a bacterial infection.
• My family has around ___ colds per year.

There is no doubt that childhood diseases hurried Mozart's early death, particularly his many streptococcal infections.

Who has had chicken pox in your class? Talk about its predecessor, smallpox, which once claimed the lives of 9 out of 10 its victims.

The Courts of Europe

Bring in a picture book on the castles of Europe. Today crowds of tourists visit the very castles that Leopold described in his letters. Nonetheless, the days of these sovereigns were numbered:

– France: Two years after Mozart's death, the king and queen of France were beheaded.
– England: Mozart was 20 when the England lost the United States in 1776.

- Has anyone in your class been to Europe, or seen a movie set in a European city?
- How does it differ in appearance from North American cities?
- Find a map of Europe and have your students trace Mozart's Grand Tour.

Gifts, Toys and Inventions

In bygone days, toys were often based on adult luxuries. For example, Mozart was given gold toothpick-cases, ribbons, watches, music boxes and tortoise-shell snuff boxes as presents for playing at court.

   Questions to ask:

- What are your favorite toys? How many are based on television or movie characters?
- Does anyone have a music box they can bring into class? Look at its playing mechanism and investigate it.
  – How do you get different pitches? [Answer: different lengths of the teeth on the "comb."]
  – What turns the barrel? [Answer: a metal spring.]
- How do watches of olden days differ from ours? [Answers: They use springs, not batteries, and have digital displays, not analogue faces.] Note that watches play an important role in this recording. Karl notices that his watch is going backwards. A poignant anecdote: during the last weeks of his life, Mozart lay in bed counting out the acts of *The Magic Flute*, which was playing to packed houses several blocks away.

Backwardsland

Leopold's bedtime story is based on the fact that Mozart loved to pass the long travel hours drawing maps and pictures of an imaginary country called Rücken (Backwardsland). In it, "he was king and the people loyal and good."

   Questions to ask:

- Do you have an imaginary friend or kingdom?
- Draw a map of an imaginary land. Mark in ponds, forests, mountains, paths and houses.
- Mozart was an expert in two ways of speaking backwards. Try these techniques:
  – Ask a friend to say a sentence, then repeat it backwards. For example, "I want to go outside and play" becomes, "Play and outside go to want I."
  – Reverse the letters in each word. For example, Wolfgang Mozart often signed his letters "Gnagflow Trazom." Write out your name backwards and see if you can pronounce it.

Genius

Ask the children:

- How would you define genius?
- Do you know anyone — a friend or even a brother or sister — whom you would call a genius? Is that person generous or conceited, solitary or sociable?
- What atheletes, singers or actors would you consider to be geniuses?

- Both Mozart and Beethoven died in relative poverty. Should popular figures be compensated with the huge sums of money they receive today?
- What do you think is the meaning of this quotation: "Talent does what it can, genius what it must"?
- Consider screening the films *Good Will Hunting* and *Searching for Bobby Fischer.* Both films depict young geniuses who, as Leopold said, "just seem to know things without being taught."

Exploring the Music

Overture to The Marriage of Figaro

It would be difficult to find a more exciting opening to an opera!

- Let your younger students run off some steam with this sizzling movement.
- Analyze this piece with your students. Write this description on the board and have your students raise their hands when they hear the following:
  - Agitated violins — in which register? [Answer: lower.]
  - The winds take over — which ones? [Answer: flute and clarinets.]
  - The violins eagerly take over again. [Answer: higher register.]
  - Contrast this to the Horn Concerto in terms of rhythm. [Answer: the opening horn concerto is in triplets; this in quadruplet 16th notes.]
- Listen to the highlights of *The Marriage of Figaro (Le nozze di Figaro):* the Overture, the "Canzonetta sull' aria," "Non so piu," "Dove sono" and "Deh vieni." In this wonderful opera, the love interest is lightly handled, making it ideal for young people.

Child's Minuet in C

Listen to the Minuet in the background of the court scene and ask the children:

- What is its time signature? [Answer: 3/4.]
- Play it on recorders and piano.
- Teach your class how to dance the minuet using either this piece or Bach's Minuet in G. When your students understand the footwork, have them dance in pairs with fingertips touching, as if a large skirt is keeping them apart. Elegant, classy and simple to do!

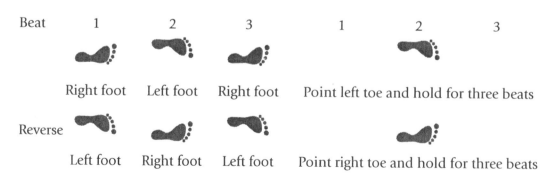

Beat	1	2	3	1	2	3
	Right foot	Left foot	Right foot	Point left toe and hold for three beats		
Reverse	Left foot	Right foot	Left foot	Point right toe and hold for three beats		

- Replace toe-pointing with curtseying and bowing.
- Ask your students how this minuet differs from today's dances in terms of tempo and style.

Children's Minuet

Composing Using Dice

People in Mozart's time often played a musical composition game using dice. Each number on the dice was associated with a written musical phrase. Players would throw the dice and piece together a minuet based on the numbers.

- You can find instructions on how to do this on the Internet at *http://204.96.11.210/ jchuang/Music/Mozart/mozart.cgi.*

Symphony No. 1, First Movement

When Leopold caught a cold in London, Mozart was forbidden to practice so as not to wake his father. He amused himself by composing this first symphony. What confident, spirited writing we find by this eight-year-old marvel!

- Listen again to the opening movement and ask your class to describe each phrase. Alternatively, list these elements on the chalkboard in a mixed-up order and ask your students to arrange them as they occur in Mozart's piece.
  - Loud violins in unison on a chord
  - Soft answering phrase — played by which instrument? [Answer: horns.]
  - Repeated phrases
  - Descending scale
  - Accented ascending phrase
  - Gentle violin dance
  - Syncopated dance
  - Forceful ascending scales
  - Coda (short answering phrases)

- Ask your students to identify the key signature. [Answer: 4/4.]
- Have them conduct it, first indicating only the beats with their arms and then indicating the dynamics and phrasings with their hands and bodies (conducting!).

Variations on "Là ci Darem"

As we shall see in the last scene, Beethoven worshipped Mozart. He wrote several sets of variations on Mozart's operatic arias, including this wonderful piece from *Don Giovanni*.

Questions to ask and activities to suggest:

- What instruments are playing here? [Answer: two oboes and bassoon.]
- Make up some words to reflect its arch, humorous restraint.
- Sing or play it on recorders as written here.
- Experiment with interpretation, performing it in different ways: slower–faster, louder–softer. Which do you prefer?

Flute Quartet: Orchestration

Listen to the quiet-breathing second movement of the Flute Quartet in D (K. 285).

- Help the children expand their vocabulary by asking them to find interpretive adjectives for this performance. [Examples: slow, peaceful, magic, singing.]
- Ask your students how Mozart achieves this mood. [Answer: plucked strings set against smooth long lines of eloquent flute.]
- Suggest some pictures to draw: the moon reflected on a still lake, an owl in a tree, a teddy bear at rest.

SCENE 3: ITALY AND A WEDDING

LENGTH OF SCENE: 13:08   TAPE STARTING POINT: SIDE 2/9:05   CD TRACKS 11–18

BEGINS: *"Come on, I want to see more of his life!"*
ENDS: *"Your guard of honor is ready to escort you."*

The Story

Karl and the Dream Children travel five years forward in time to see Mozart on his Italian trip. At 14, the young musician astonished the world by copying from memory a nine-part piece that he had heard sung only once, at the Vatican. Traveling another 12 years into the future, the Dream Children look down on Mozart's wedding day. His bride, Constanze, and her younger sister, Aloysia, are excitedly getting ready for the big event. Mozart delivers a riddle poem and the women sing a duet to the bridegroom.

The Music

- Symphony No. 40, K. 550, Mvt 1
- *Miserere Mei*, by Allegri
- Cassation in C, K. 63
- Minuet, *Don Giovanni*, K. 527
- Barrel-Organ Variation on "Deh vieni," *Don Giovanni*, K. 527
- Variations on "Ah, vous dirai-je, madame," K. 265
- Letter Duet ("Canzonetta sull' aria"), *The Marriage of Figaro*, K. 265

Note: Unfortunately the tape-divide is in the middle of this scene. Please turn over the tape and listen to about nine minutes of Side 2.

Background Information

Trip to Italy (1766)

This scene opens with the famous incident in which 14-year-old Mozart astonished everyone by writing out the notes to Allegri's *Miserere* after hearing it sung only once. To give an idea of this achievement, consider that this is a 15-minute piece composed of nine separate voices. It is sung in the Sistine Chapel Choir only at Easter.

In Rome, the Vatican functioned much like a royal court, enforcing dress rules on Sunday and making sure that nobody broke church rules on Lent or saints' days. Someone once said that "in Rome, even the cats go to church"!

Musical Genius

Ask your class to think back a few years to when they were young. Outline these early signs of Mozart's genius.

- At three, Mozart would climb up on the piano bench after Nannerl's lesson and pick out thirds (C to E). Soon he was learning Nannerl's piano pieces for two hands in just half an hour.

- At four, Mozart tried to compose his first piano concerto. Leopold and a friend discovered him writing out a smudged but legible score. When they commented that it was hard to perform, Mozart played it, declaring, "That's why it's a concerto. You must practice hard to play a concerto."
- At five, Mozart picked up a violin and played it without ever having had a lesson. The story goes that once when Leopold had some friends over to play music, his son begged to join them. The child then effortlessly played along at sight, claiming, "It's not hard to play because it's only the *second* violin."
- Mozart named his first instrument his "butter violin" because of its sweet tone. So keen was his sense of pitch that he could tell if a violin was even one-eighth of a tone out of tune. (Remember that a piano is tuned only in half tones — demonstrate this on a piano if possible.) The child was equally sensitive to loud instruments, and would run from the room to escape the sound of a trumpet.

Constanze Weber

Leopold disapproved heartily of Mozart's marriage into the musical Weber family, which was composed of a strong mother and four gifted daughters. Mozart first loved Aloysia, who married someone else; then he turned to Constanze. The oldest sister, Josepha, sang the Queen of the Night in *The Magic Flute*, and the youngest, Sophie, cared for him in his final illness.

Mozart's Adult Life in Vienna

The year 1784 was an important one for Mozart: it was the year of the birth of Karl and the death of his father. Mozart also broke off all contact with his sister, Nannerl, because she shared Leopold's negative view of his marriage. He had lost his mother six years earlier when she accompanied him on a Parisian trip to help him find a court appointment.

As the center of the "Classical style" (Haydn, Mozart and Beethoven), Vienna was a flourishing royal city. Civic life thrived in elegant coffee houses. In the magnificent public gardens, deer grazed under chestnut trees and music spilled from pavillions. In winter, horses decked with silver bells pulled ornate sleighs through the streets, followed by squads of torchbearers and musicians (similar to Handel's Water Music on the river Thames. See the Classical Kids recording *Hallelujah Handel!*). For all this grandeur, the residents of Vienna often complained of clouds of dust kicked up by horse's hoofs in the unbearable summer heat.

Mozart, Math and Spatial Reasoning

Mozart loved math and, as a child, covered the tables, chairs, walls and floors of his room with numbers. Once, while on an Italian trip, he begged Nannerl to send him some lost math tables. Many educators now suggest that listening to Mozart improves math and spatial reasoning (see Don Campbell's book and recordings, *The Mozart Effect*).

Mozart also loved to play billiards with Constanze at home. Billiards requires spatial and multi-layered thinking, like music, which weaves horizontal melodies together with vertical chords.

Discussion and Activities

To capture the exotic flavor of Italy, bring in some tourist books. Read this description of Naples' famous "Passagio": "At night, aristocrats drive their carriages along the Adriatic, torches flaming and liveried servants running alongside; Mount Vesuvius smokes furiously in the background."

• Play some royal music by Mozart or Handel, and ask your students to draw this scene.

Of Lice and Mice: Fashion and Customs in the 18th Century

For people like Mozart who loved to dress up, the 18th century was a delicious circus! Research the history of fashion. Look at this picture of a lady's wig from France. Some wigs were so high that they had a lever inside so that ladies could lower the wig when they entered a carriage. Here are some questions:

• What were wigs made of? [Answer: human hair and horse hair.]

• Why were wigs white? [Answer: flour or lead compound was blown onto the hair by servants in the "powder room" — a name we still use today.]

• How did the powder stick to the wig? [Answer: with pig's fat. Imagine the smell of rancid fat — perhaps that's why perfume was invented in France!]

• Were wigs itchy? [Answer: Yes. The 18th century was the "century of scratching." At elegant dinners, a silver claw was often placed at each setting for scratching the lice, which thrived on the flour and pig fat in the wigs.]

• Show pictures of dress from the 18th century and ask students:
  – How did they make the ladies dresses so wide? [Answer: "Panniers," basket-like contraptions, were strapped around the waist and padded with straw. They frequently became infested with mice.]

- Measure your waist. Then make a 17-inch (43-centimeter) circle with your hands by leaving about 6 inches (15 centimeters) between your finger tips. This was the preferred waist size for women in Mozart's time. Women were strapped into corsets strengthened with whale bone. Not only did these garments hamper breathing and make ladies swoon, but they also reduced muscle tone. Like Chinese foot-binding, corsets took away a woman's independence, because she needed maids to tug the ties tightly into place.
- Do you know why a man often walks curbside today? [Answer: It's comes from the 18th century, when a man protected his female companion's dress from the street sludge kicked up by the horses and the contents of chamber pots being emptied onto the street from the windows above.]

Exploring the Music

Mozart's Compositional Technique

Constanze wrote that "Mozart wrote down music in the same way as he wrote letters." He often composed a whole movement in his head while playing billiards or walking about town. He would then write it down later with very few changes. This method of composition is very unlike Beethoven, who worked through many drafts and produced scores scarred with violent crossings-out.

Questions to ask:

- When you write a story, what is your working style? Do you sketch out an idea to establish the setting, beginning, development and ending before you start? Or do you "discover" your own plot as you write? Do you work through many drafts?
- Which is the better technique, or can everyone have a different style?

Slurs and Violin Technique

Symphony No. 40 remains one of Mozart's most popular compositions.

- Listen here to the quick two-note phrases in the violins, called slurs. Rapid slurs give a restless urgency to the music, as here. Played slowly, slurs are more like sighs.
- Ask the children to imagine playing slurs on a violin. Would you change the bow direction during a slur? [Answer: no.]
- Invite a violinist to come into class and demonstrate bowing, slurs, vibrato, tremolo, double stops and pizzicato.

Miserere Mei, by Allegri

This 15-minute choral piece was sung only once a year by the Vatican Choir at Easter.

- Ask the children to raise a hand when they hear the highest note. Can anyone sing it?
- Bring in a picture of the Sistine Chapel and explain how it took Michelangelo four years to paint the ceiling, lying on his back. To appreciate how hard this is, ask the children to lie on the floor and "paint the air" above them for two minutes while you play some music by Mozart.

Minuet from Don Giovanni

Recorder:

Sing:

I love to dance a min-u-et, fair lad-ies in a cir-cle!

Recorder:

Dance 2

Hear them play-ing, hear them bray-ing, come and sing a song with us!

Come and sing a song with us.

Dance 3

Dance, dance, dance, dance monk-ey, prance monk-key, show us your steps!

I love to dance a min-u-et, fair lad-ies in a cir-cle

Mozart's Operas

Mozart began composing and conducting operas when he was 12 years old: *La finta semplice* (The Pretend Simpleton, written at 12), *Bastien und Bastienne* (composed at 12 and still performed today), *Mitradate* (14), *La finta giardiniera* (The Pretend Garden Girl) and *Il re pastore* (The Shepherd King, written at age 19). Mozart loved operas all his life, writing approximately 20 of them in just 35 years.

Minuet from Don Giovanni

The scene of the Dream Children cruising towards Vienna is based on the dance sequence from *Don Giovanni*. In the opera, it is wonderfully staged with three groups dancing different rhythms. This composition is so complicated that even Mozart had to sketch it out in advance.

- What is its time signature? [Answer: 3/4.]
- Split the class in three groups and do counter-clappings as notated here:

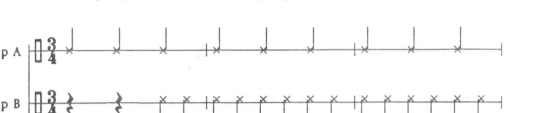

- Group A: Clap the three basic beats through the entire piece.
- Group B: Clap the rhythm of the country dance. What is it? [Answer: 2/4 in eighth notes.]
- Group C: Clap the third rhythm of the organ grinder. What is it? [Answer: 9/8 — compound.]

- Sing and play the minuet on page 26. As you can see, it has been arranged in increasing levels of difficulty. The opening minuet is the backbone that holds the composition together.
  - Sing the first page, with or without the recorder doubling the piano melody.
  - Play the same piano accompaniment and sing Dance 2 on top of it. Again, the recorder is optional.
  - Play the same piano accompaniment and sing Dance 3 on top of it. This is more difficult because you are singing three beats against two. The recorder is optional.
  - Combine all three dances in whatever manner you choose, and perform it in a school concert.

Twinkle Variations (on "Ah, vous dirai-je, madame")

Although the English-speaking world knows this melody as "Twinkle, Twinkle Little Star" or "The Alphabet Song," it first appeared in France under the title "Ah, vous dirai-je, madame." Analyze variations as follows:

- *Listening:* What does Mozart add in Variation No. 1? [Answer: fast-running 16th notes.] Listen to how this pianistic filigree wraps around the principle note and makes it sparkle like a diamond.

- *Instruments:* What advantage does a keyboard have over other instruments in playing complex pieces? [Answer: only keyboards can play many notes at a time.]

- *Analysis:* Listen to the entire nine variations and analyze how Mozart changes the theme with each repetition. [Hint: listen for variations in triple time, use of the minor key, arpeggios and scales, and crossing hands.]

- *Playing:* Play the theme and accompaniment on recorders as written here.

Ah, vous dirai-je, madame

"Canzonetta sull' aria," The Marriage of Figaro

In the original opera, the Countess is planning to meet the Count in a shaded arbor. Unfortunately, her husband loves someone else. In this duet, the Countess dictates a letter to her maid Suzanna and plans to meet her husband in the garden in disguise.

Constanze and her sister first sang this aria with Mozart at the piano. All three ended in tears. Typical of Mozart, *The Marriage of Figaro* was finished in a flurry of activity. Just days before its opening, the people of Prague were treated to watching Mozart and the librettist shouting or singing phrases out their windows across the cobbled streets.

This is one of Mozart's most beautiful compositions. Ask your students:

- What do you call a piece with two voices? [Answer: a duet.]
- What are Constanze and her sister singing about? [Answer: their feelings about marriage.]
- What is the mood of the song? [Suggestion: liltingly tender.]
- What is its rhythm? [Answer: triple time, like a lullaby.]
- What other musical devices does Mozart use? [Answer: echoing phrases, gentle violins, singing oboes.]

- Move to it, using scarves or streamers. Try to make your bodies reflect the mood and flow of the music.

SCENE 4: CONCLUSION

LENGTH OF SCENE: 10:50   TAPE STARTING POINT: SIDE 2/9:05   CD TRACKS 19–23

BEGINS: *"For better, for worse, Prince Wolfgang, your princess comes to claim you!"*
ENDS: *"Wolfgang Amadeus Mozart"*

The Story

The flying boat takes Karl and the Dream Children mysteriously forward in time. They arrive in a graveyard, where Karl meets Beethoven. The children enter a musical vortex where they hear Mozart's name called all over Europe. Landing back at the school, Karl hides the Dream Children in his closet when he hears his father arrive. After Karl and his father are reconciled, all return to a performance of *The Magic Flute*. During the final song, Mozart finishes his letter to Constanze. The recording closes with a quiet piano piece with no words to give listeners time to reflect on the story.

The Music:

- Eine kleine Nachtmusik, K. 525, Mvt 4
- Ave Verum Corpus, K. 618
- Waldstein Sonata, Op. 53, by Beethoven
- Piano Concerto in C, K. 459, Mvt 1
- Piano Sonata in A, K. 331, Mvt 1
- Gran Partita, K. 361, Mvt 7
- "Blow Softly, You Breezes" ("Soave sia il vento"), *Così fan tutte*, K. 588
- Piano Sonata in A, K. 331, Mvt 1

Background

Mozart's Last Summer and Fall

In the winter of 1791, the world was blissfully unaware that it was about to lose one of its greatest composers. Here is the sequence of events for Mozart's last six months.

- June 2: Mozart moves into the hut near Vienna's Freihaus Opera House located on an island in the Danube river. The eccentric producer Emanuel Schikenader built this house for Mozart to live in while he composed *The Magic Flute*.
- Meanwhile, Constanze and Karl pass the hot summer days at the baths of Baden, a spa town near Vienna. Mozart often visits them and finishes Ave Verum Corpus there on June 17.
- July 26: Constanze returns to Vienna for the birth of Franz Xavier.
- August 26: Karl goes back to school while his parents go to Prague to see a performance of *La Clemenza di Tito*.
- September 21: Karl's birthday. On September 30, he is taken by the composer Salieri and Mozart to see *The Magic Flute*. He stays over a day for a special dinner with his father, then returns to school from a trip.
- November 30: Mozart is dying of a strange liver ailment. The youngest Weber sister, Sophie, looks after him until Constanze returns.

Mozart's Early Death

Mozart died on December 21, 1791, at the age of 35 years, 11 months and 9 days. Beethoven always believed Mozart's claim that he was being poisoned. It is, however, more likely that Mozart died of a liver ailment and rheumatic fever, possibly brought on by overwork and the many childhood diseases that had weakened him.

Only eight people followed the snowy funeral procession to the cemetery where Mozart was unceremoniously dumped into a common grave. Neither Constanze nor their sons attended, but this was not uncommon, because the funeral service had already taken place in the church.

Beethoven

Unlike Mozart, Beethoven did not have an easy relationship with his father. Beethoven's father said: "What stupid stuff are you scraping at now? You know I can't stand hearing it! Play the notes in front of you, or all your scrapings will amount to nothing!" Imagine Leopold saying such a thing!

Beethoven worshipped Mozart all his life. At 17, he traveled to Vienna in the hopes of studying with the 31-year old Mozart. The composer was impressed, saying, "Watch this young man, for he shall make a great noise in the world some day." Unfortunately, Beethoven's mother died and he had to return to Bonn to take care of his alcoholic father. By the time he returned to Vienna, Mozart was dead and the young man studied with Haydn instead. It was said at the time that "Beethoven received the spirit of Mozart from the hands of Haydn."

To appreciate the contrasts between Mozart and Beethoven, reread the opening Letter to Teachers. While Beethoven was unkempt, negligent, moody, reclusive and dreamy, Mozart was fastidious, buoyant, sociable and very pragmatic. Mozart struggled all his life to get a princely appointment; Beethoven defiantly declared, "There are many princes, but there is only *one* Beethoven!" Beethoven was helped in this independence by the rise of the middle class, the proliferation of pianos in private houses, the building of public concert halls and the publishing possibilities resulting from all of these developments.

An interesting link between Mozart and Beethoven was Prince Karl Lichnowsky (the prince mentioned in the Classical Kids recording *Beethoven Lives Upstairs*). Born in the same year as Mozart, Lichnowsky became Mozart's pupil and later patron. In 1789, he arranged for Mozart to accompany him to Leipzig to see the church and writings of Johann Sebastian Bach. Imagine, about 50 years after Bach's death, Mozart spreading out his scores and excitedly exclaiming, "Now, *here's* something I can learn from!" The prince later took Beethoven on a similar trip and was richly rewarded: Beethoven's dedicated his famous "Pathètique" Piano Sonata (Op. 13) to Prince Karl Lichnowsky.

Beethoven played Mozart's Piano Concerto K. 466 at Mozart's memorial concert, and asked that Mozart's Requiem be played at his own funeral.

What Happened to Constanze?

History has dealt critically with Constanze for her flightiness and failure to be by her husband during his dying days. Left destitute at his death, she energetically arranged a series of concerts to raise funds for her sons. The boys sometimes participated in these concerts.

> PRAGUE CONCERT, NOVEMBER 15, 1797
> By special request, little Wolfgang,
> just six years old and the younger of Mozart's bereaved children,
> will give a small token of his respectful thanks to the worthy public of Prague
> for its affection towards is father, displayed here so many times;
> he will demonstrate his growing desire
> to emulate his father's example by singing the aria
> from Die Zauberflöte [The Magic Flute], "der Vogelfanger."
> Indulgence is pleaded for this first expression of his tender talent.

It is Constanze and her second husband, Nissen, whom we have to thank for the publication of 500 of Mozart's works, left lying around the house after his death. (Only 70 were published during Mozart's lifetime.) Nissen also wrote a biography of the composer. When he died, Constanze returned to Salzburg, where she lived just blocks away from Nannerl, but the two women seldom spoke.

What Happened to Karl?

Karl was reasonably musical and even composed a bit. He later became an accountant in northern Italy. By this time, sufficient income was coming in from his father's estate for him to be independently wealthy. He donated many scores to the Mozart museum in Salzburg and died in 1858 at the age of 74.

Discussion and Activities

Science: Sound Effects and New Instruments

The "vortex" ("Help me, help me, help me") at the end of the graveyard scene took over eight hours of studio time to create.

- Ask the children to identify what they hear in this segment. [Answers: music, thunder, an explosion, voices that have been put in a replicating chamber.] Always fascinated with theatrical effects, Mozart would probably have loved these technologies!

Four Endings

The conclusion of any story must resolve the fate of the central characters and give the central theme. Ask your students to tell what happens in each of these scenes:

- The graveyard scene with Beethoven. [Answer: We find out that Mozart dies soon but that his music lives on.]
- The school scene. [Answer: It solves Karl's problem with his father and the Dream Children's problem in the opera.]
- The letter scene. [Answer: Mozart hints at his approaching death and his belief in music. He tells us that Karl is doing better.]
- The last quiet piano piece. [Answer: It serves as a reflective time for us to think about what has happened.]

Creative Writing: Letters and Other Literary Devices

Mozart's Magnificent Voyage brackets the central action between two letters written by Mozart to Constanze. They poetically set up the problem and resolution.

- Ask the children to put the content in their own words.
  - The first letter says that Mozart is writing *The Magic Flute* in the summer hut, that he is away from his family and Karl is in trouble, and that he doesn't know what to do with the Dream Children.
  - In the last letter, Mozart describes the success of the opera and describes Karl happily trading jokes with the Dream Children. He hints at his own death with "I do not know what is going to happen, but for now let the music be our guide."
- Take something you have already written and recast it in letter form.
- Change the point of view to build the story around a different character. For example, if it is about a boy and his dog, rewrite it from the point of view of the dog.
- What other literary devices are used in *Mozart's Magnificent Voyage*? [Answer: alternating real-time scenes with magical time travel.]
- Give examples of each type of scene. [Answer: Sailing in the boat is magical. There are five real-time scenes: Karl's room, court, the Vatican, Mozart's wedding, the graveyard.]

Exploring the Music

Eine kleine Nachtmusik

No recording about Mozart would be complete without a movement from this well-known piece. In fame, it is equivalent to Vivaldi's "The Four Seasons" or Beethoven's "Ode to Joy." Written in 1787 for strings only, Eine kleine Nachtmusik fairly bubbles with life. It is a rondo, which means that the opening theme keeps returning with new material between each of its statements.

- Play the whole rondo and ask students to raise a hand when they hear the theme return.
- Listen to the whole piece again and count how often the theme returns. [Answer: four.]

Two Religious Works: Ave Verum Corpus and the Requiem

Although he was very ill, Mozart wrote an astonishing amount of music in his last year: this lovely Ave Verum Corpus, *The Magic Flute*, *La Clemenza di Tito* (a full opera), the Clarinet Concerto for Stadler, the Requiem and a piano concerto. The Requiem was commissioned by a stranger who probably wanted to claim it as his own. Like Beethoven, Haydn asked that it be sung at his funeral.

- Show the film *Amadeus* to your class to explore the story of the Requiem.

Mozart and the Piano

Although Mozart could play the violin, he was most famous as a pianist. His piano concerti and 18 sonatas are among his most popular compositions. In this recording, the piano sonority represents Karl: his early rage in his room, and his reconciliation with his father late in the recording. This last piece is a lovely set of variations rocking gently in three.

- Play it on the recorder as written here.

Sonata

"Blow Softly, You Breezes" ("Soave sia il vento"), Così fan tutte

In the opera *Così fan tutte*, this trio depicts a boat pulling away from the shore propelled by a sweet wind.

- Have students draw this scene, or whatever else it suggests to them.
- How does Mozart create the sensation of floating? [Answer: tenderly swaying violins support the high voices in thirds.]

Mozart and the Classical Kids Series

Mozart's story intersects with almost every other composer covered in the Classical Kids Series of recordings:

- *Vivaldi's Ring of Mystery:* Mozart and Vivaldi are both buried in the same Viennese cemetery.
- *Mr. Bach Comes to Call:* After Mozart saw Bach's compositions near the end of his life, he began to use fugues in his own works. As a child in London, he befriended Bach's youngest son, Johann Christian.
- *Beethoven Lives Upstairs:* Beethoven worshipped Mozart and wanted to study with him.
- *Mozart's Magic Fantasy:* The three Dream Children here are drawn from this recording.
- *Tchaikovsky Discovers America:* Tchaikovsky imitated Mozart's clear orchestrations and said: "When I play Mozart, I feel brighter and younger, almost youthful again... To my mind, Mozart is the culminating point of all beauty in the sphere of music. He alone can make me weep and tremble with delight."
- *Hallelujah Handel:* Mozart wrote new instrumentation for Handel's Messiah. This is the form in which we most often hear this timeless piece. Both Handel and Mozart were great travelers who loved London.

After the Recording

Questions to ask:

- Talk about the title of this recording with the class. Can you figure out two ways in which this recording depicts a voyage? [Answer: Karl and the Dream Children travel through time, Mozart travels through his life.]

- Write or draw the scenes you remember on separate sheets of paper. Arrange them on the wall in order to tell the story. Alternatively, create a group mural using visual elements from *Mozart's Magnificent Voyage.*
- What new facts have you learned about Mozart?
- Divide a blank page in two and label one column "Fiction," the other one "Fact." Sort out which is which based on the recording and your subsequent discussions in class.
- Retell the story in your own words or make a storyboard.
- Research and make a project about Mozart's life and music.

CLASSICAL KIDS AND THE INTEGRATED CURRICULUM

This chart and the following 10-day Lesson Plan illustrate the themes and skills developed in these Teacher's Notes for *Mozart's Magnificent Voyage.*

There is also a sample question sheet after the Lesson Plan for those teachers wishing to assess their students' skills and knowledge with a short test.

Core Area	Mozart
Time Frame	1756–1791
Geography	Austria
Social Studies	• European courts • Wigs, fashion • Games, toys, pets
Creative Writing	• Time travel • Real time and magic time • Writing letters • Storyboards • Retelling the story • Fact and fiction • Backwardsland
Modern Issues	• Prodigies, genius • Father–son relations • Life without school
Other Arts	• Painting murals • Sound effects • Architecture • Dance
Music	• Analyzing excerpts • Playing and singing • Interpreting vocabulary • Conducting • Playing minuets • Biography
Math and Science	• Inventions • Medicine, disease • Math and music • Vortex

Suggested Lesson Plan

Week One

MONDAY	TUESDAY	WEDNESDAY	THURSDAY	FRIDAY
Side One Introducing the Characters • Karl (7) • Dream Children (7) **Journeys** • Title (6) • Time travel (9)	**Side Two Modern Issues** • Life without school (9) • Prodigies (6, 17) • Talking backwards (17) • Backwardsland (17) **Other Arts** • Sound effects (9) • Vortex (33)	**Biography** • Young life (8) • Genius (22) • Pets and toys (8) • Grand Tour (14) • Trip to Italy (23) • Last year (31) • Early death (32) • Beethoven (32) • Constanze (32) • Karl (33) **Creative Writing** • Letters (15, 33) • Real-time/magic time (6, 34) • Time travel (34) • Storyboard/ retelling story (36)	**Other Arts** • Casting and vocal technique (9) **Visual arts** • Drawing magic boat (9) • Painting imaginary kingdom (17) • Painting to Flute Quartet (20) • Painting mural (36) • Drawing scenes and arranging order (36)	**Music: Singing** • Horn Concerto (10) • "Oragnia Fitafagnia Fa" (10) **Music: Analysis** • Clarinet Quintet (10) • Symphony No. 1, Mvt 1 (20) • Symphony No. 1, Mvt 2 (11) • Eine kleine Nachtmusik (34) • Figaro overture (18) • "Canzonetta Sull' aria" (30) • "Blow softly" (36)

Week Two

MONDAY	TUESDAY	WEDNESDAY	THURSDAY	FRIDAY
Music: Singing • "Three Spirits" (12) • *Miserere* (25) • Composing techniques (25) **Alternative** • Movies: *Amadeus, Searching for Bobby Fisher, Good Will Hunting* (36)	**Music: Recorder** • Là ci Darem (20) • "Twinkle, Twinkle" (29) • Piano Sonata (35) **Alternative** • Movies cont'd	**Science** • Disease (16) • Gifts and toys (17) • Math and billiards (24) **Social History** • Castles (17) • Vienna (24) • Wigs (24) • Panniers (25)	**Minuet Day** • Playing Minuet in C (18) • Dancing to Minuet in C (19) • Making minuets with dice (19) • Minuet from *Don Giovanni*: clapping counter-rhythms (26–28)	**Finishing Up** • Four endings (33) • Requiem (34) • Classical Kids and other composers (36) • Review (36) • Fact and fiction (36) • Worksheet (39)

Worksheet for Mozart's Magnificent Voyage

1. Mozart was born in the year _____.
   He died in _____ at the age of ___.
2. He lived in the country of _____
3. His father was named _____ .
   His sister was named _____ .
4. What pets did Mozart have? What games
   did he play? _____
   _____
   _____
5. The Grand Tour lasted _____ years,
   from when Mozart was age ___ to ____.
6. Name three countries they visited:_____
   _____
   _____
7. What extraordinary thing did Mozart do in
   Rome? _____
   _____
8. Why was Mozart called "the little magician"?
   _____
   _____
   _____
9. What are the names of Mozart's two children?
   _____
10. What is the name of Mozart's wife?
    _____
11. Why is Karl upset? _____
    _____
    _____
12. The Dream Children come from which
    opera? _____
13. Why are the Dream Children upset?
    _____
    _____
14. How do Karl and the Dream Children
    travel?_____
    _____

15. Name two classical composers who loved
    Mozart. _____
    _____
16. What did Mozart say about Beethoven as a
    young man? _____
    _____
17. What is Backwardsland? _____
    _____
18. Write your name backwards._____
    _____
19. On what famous tune did Mozart write
    variations? _____
20. Wigs in the 18th century were colored with
    _____ held on by _____.
    They have lots of _____ in them.
21. Ladies wide skirts are held out with
    _____. Their waists are held in with
    _____ to make them look ____ inches/
    centimeters.
22. What does Karl come to realize during this
    recording? _____
    _____
    _____
23. Use some adjectives to describe the last duet.
    _____
    _____
24. In your own words, tell the story of *Mozart's
    Magnificent Voyage.* _____
    _____
    _____
    _____
25. What was your favorite scene? _____
    _____
26. What was your favorite piece of music?
    _____

ANSWERS: Cut this portion off before photocopying. (1) 1756, 1791, 35; (2) Austria; (3) Leopold, Nannerl; (4) dogs, birds, fish, grasshoppers; playing with hobby horse, drawing imaginary maps; (5) 3; (6) France, England, Holland; (7) wrote the 9-part Miserere *from memory after hearing it once; (8) he had perfect pitch, could play any piece with the keys covered; (9) Karl, Franz Xavier; (10) Constanze; (11) he hates his boarding school and his father is coming to reprimand him; (12) The Magic Flute; (13) Mozart is going to write them out of the opera; (14) by magic flying boat; (15) Beethoven, Haydn; (16) "Watch this young man for he shall make a great noise in the world one day"; (17) an imaginary land that Mozart made up; (18) N/A; (19) "Twinkle, Twinkle Little Star"; (20) flour and lead, pig's fat, lice; (21) panniers, corsets, 17"/43 cm; (22) that his father loves him, that he will always have his music; (23) peaceful, floating; (24) Dream Children and Karl fly inn a magic boat above Europe to look down on Mozart, Karl meets Beethoven and is united with his father; (25) N/A; (26) N/A*

Beethoven Lives Upstairs

AUDIO: Juno Award Best Children's Recording (Canada), Parents' Choice Silver Honor (U.S.), American Library Association Notable Children's Recording Award, Practical Home Schooling Reader Award Music Curriculum Category and Educational Audio Cassette Category (U.S.), Film Advisory Board Award of Excellence (U.S.), Parents' Choice Classic Award (U.S.), Certified Gold Record (Canada), Certified Platinum Record (Canada)

BOOK: Governor General's Award Finalist – Illustration (Canada), Canadian Children's Book Centre Our Choice Recommendation

VIDEO: Emmy Award for Best Children's Program, Parents' Choice Movie Hall of Fame Classic and Gold Awards (U.S.), Dove Foundation Dove Family Approved Seal, Oppenheim Toy Portfolio Platinum Award (U.S.), Film Advisory Board Award of Excellence (U.S.), Gold Camera Award Best Children's Program and Best Direction (U.S.), Certified Multi-Platinum Video (Canada)

CD-ROM: National Parenting Publications Honors Award (U.S.), Film Advisory Board Award of Excellence (U.S.), Curriculum Administrator Top 100 Districts' Choice Award (U.S.)

Mr. Bach Comes to Call

Parents' Choice Gold Award (U.S.), American Library Association Notable Children's Recording Award, Parents' Choice Classic Award (U.S.), Practical Home Schooling Reader Award Music Curriculum Category and Educational Audio Cassette Category (U.S.), Film Advisory Board Award of Excellence (U.S.), Certified Gold Record (Canada), Certified Platinum Record (Canada)

Tchaikovsky Discovers America

AUDIO: Juno Award Best Children's Recording (Canada), American Library Association Notable Children's Recording Award, Parents' Choice Classic Award (U.S.), Practical Home Schooling Reader Award Music Curriculum Category and Educational Audio Cassette Category (U.S.), Audio File Earphones Award of Excellence (U.S.), Certified Gold Record (Canada)

BOOK: Canadian Children's Book Centre Our Choice Recommendation, Gibbon Award Finalist Illustration (Canada)

Mozart's Magic Fantasy

Juno Award Best Children's Recording (Canada), Parents' Choice Gold Award, American Library Association Notable Children's Recording Award, Parents' Choice Classic Award (U.S.), Practical Home Schooling Reader Award Music Curriculum Category and Educational Audio Cassette Category (U.S.), Film Advisory Board Award of Excellence (U.S.), Certified Gold Record (Canada), Certified Platinum Record (Canada)

Vivaldi's Ring of Mystery

Juno Award Best Children's Recording (Canada), Parent's Choice Gold Award (U.S.), American Library Association Notable Children's Recording Award, Parents' Choice Classic Award (U.S.), Practical Home Schooling Reader Award Music Curriculum Category and Educational Audio Cassette Category (U.S.), Audio File Earphones Award of Excellence (U.S.), Film Advisory Board Award of Excellence (U.S.), Certified Gold Recording (Canada)

Daydreams & Lullabies

Film Advisory Board Award of Excellence (U.S.), Practical Home Schooling Reader Award Music Curriculum Category and Educational Audio Cassette Category (U.S.)

Hallelujah Handel!

Parent's Choice Gold Award (U.S.), Film Advisory Board Award of Excellence (U.S.), Practical Home Schooling Reader Award Music Curriculum Category and Educational Audio Cassette Category (U.S.)

Educational Awards

Curriculum Administrator Top 100 Districts' Choice Award, Learning Magazine – Teacher's Choice Award, Practical Home Schooling Association Notable Children's Recordings

The Classroom Collection

Teacher's Choice Award Learning Magazine

Susan Hammond, Classical Kids Producer

The Order of Canada for her contribution to arts and education in Canada